To Hell with Paradise

GARETH REEVES studied at the University of Oxford and at Stanford University, where he held a Wallace Stegner Writing Fellowship. He is currently part-time Reader in English at Durham University, where he runs an MA creative writing course in poetry. Carcanet Press have published two previous collections of his poetry, *Real Stories* (1984) and *Listening In* (1993). He is also the author of two books on T.S. Eliot, a book on poetry of the 1930s (with Michael O'Neill), and many essays on nineteenth- and twentieth-century English, American and Irish poetry.

T0294075

GARETH REEVES

To Hell with Paradise

New and Selected Poems

CARCANET

Acknowledgements

Acknowledgements are due to the following publications, in which some of the poems in this book first appeared:

Agenda, Arvon International Poetry Competition: 1987 Anthology (Arvon Foundation, 1989), *Critical Quarterly, Encounter, From Wordsworth to Stevens: In Honour of Robert Rehder* (Peter Lang, 2005), *The Honest Ulsterman, Literary Review, London Review of Books, London Magazine, Makaris, New Statesman, New Walk, North by North-East* (Iron Press, 2006), *Outposts, PN Review, Times Literary Supplement.*

'Church Wall' was broadcast on BBC Radio 3.

First published in Great Britain in 2012 by

Carcanet Press Limited
Alliance House
Cross Street
Manchester M2 7AQ

www.carcanet.co.uk

Copyright © Gareth Reeves 2012

A CIP catalogue record for this book is available from the British Library

ISBN 978 1 84777 144 5

The publisher acknowledges financial assistance from Arts Council England

Typeset by XL Publishing Services, Tiverton
Printed and bound in England by SRP Ltd, Exeter

Contents

from REAL STORIES (1984)

NEW POEMS

Airs

I

Clearing the gutters:
the surprise
of leaf skeleton,

intricate bird-bone,
skein of rib-cage,
delicate eviscerations

– friable, porous,
to no purpose except
the mind's distraction.

II

Shrink until you are
beside yourself
looking ecstatically down
on times before

the talk set in,
the forevers, nevers, maybes,
the buts, ands, if-onlys,
the conjunctions and conjurations.

III

It may be too early to begin this,
it may be too late,
it may be over,
it may not have started:

words that haunt, precisely,
with an uncertain music, not to be
unsaid or said again
in any idiom. Ungainsayable.

Nothing will take the words back.

IV

Feathery constructions
of breathless air float
in the mind's eye,

roving unstoppably
to undreamt-of horizons,
lands of speculation.

They do not compromise.
They say over and over
we are here, we are here.

V

Shaping themselves
to clouds that mount
in perpetual transport,

pellucid opacities,
giving a body
to nothing that lives

except in the head.

VI

Nothing that lives in the head
lives, or dies. Nothing
will take its place.

Conduct a music
of stolen airs,
you have nothing to lose.

Lost haunt of the intimate:
it comes over you daily,
undreamt indifference,

burgeoning inhospitalities,
unsayable vows,
uncertainties so pronounced

they leave no room for denial
— except retreat
back to the self, dark chamber
of self-preservation and regard.

VII

That give delight and hurt not.
Some hope.
That work themselves up

into a semblance of bitter sense,
scurried fantasias,
arrogant, uncompromising,

becoming their own distraction,
getting their own back,
running riot, thrusting, insistent,

unequivocally
barbed and bristling,
fertile, almost familiar.

VIII

Go on, give yourself airs:

I put on airs, you put on airs,
he puts on airs, she puts on airs.
Go on, conjugate it,

dress the words up,
the little bursts and flourishes,
the forevers and I love yous,

in sharp suits, in stealthy lingerie.
Put them on, give them
a new lease, watch them
take on a life of their own.

IX

The scenario is not
played out, it is not over,
it never is, it is forever, for
ever. What is that *for*
for, what is it doing?

Say what you will
the shemozzle doesn't settle,
the dust never settles,
it is unsettling, it is moving,
it moves to its own tempo,

it comes and it goes like this,
it flies off at a tangent,
then for no reason it comes up close

to sit on my shoulder and parrot
things it has got
but not by heart.

X

Rest assured, this is a put-on,
a way of saying the things people say
without meaning much

except the sense you make
of yourself to yourself.
Sink into them,
sink your teeth into them.

XI

No use now giving yourself airs,
no use now taking a deep breath,
no use now gasping for air,
no use now going with the knowing air

– and no use summoning the vacuities,
the blank circle tightens its grip:

you cannot take
anything back, things said,
unsaid, could have said,

pregnant pauses,
sterile silences, resistancies,
they are not yours now.

Keep them, give them away: you cannot.
They are not even yours to forget.

The Shape of Pain

What figure has the pain of the toothache, and our remembrance of that pain?
Is it triangular, or circular, or of a square form?
James Beattie, *Dissertations Moral and Critical* (1783)

Every day it gets a little less.
Wait for the vanishing point.

Parallels reach for infinity.
It goes on gnawing at the edge.

Somewhere out there it stops, it must.
Out there the blue intensifies.

Tomorrow remember it today.
Today imagine it tomorrow.

Look forward to the backward look.
Every day it grows a little less:

I want it and I do not want it to.
I give it a shape. I give it this.

Azure

You dare not say what happened,
it is not finished

or so you like to think.
Watch the vapour trail
slice the sky slowly, then

dissolve to a spine
of puff-blooms in
an extravaganza of desire,

and say precisely when
the last fleck fades
to nothing, if you can.

To be possibly
the object of no
speculation, to see

yourself reduced to
untraceable episodes,

a deep breath
in the air of denial,

in the azure absolute,
is a release,
a sort of life, if you will.

Absolute

These words for you,
these words instead of you,

in anticipation
of their rejection,

that they may return
to their owner pure

as when they set out,
unsullied by understanding.

We are as we are
they say, standing for

nothing but ourselves,
so do not read us, do not say us,

do not sing us, do not
show us to anyone,

that in isolation we may hold on
to whatever it is we know, barely

content but unflinching
in our absolution,

compensation
for you
instead of you.

Lost Clusters

If I could say this to you
there would be no need to.
I say it to myself therefore.

Therefore is a difficult word for
it speaks of after and before.

Now is the time therefore
to see it, say it, therefore
the dawn still gives of itself,

the sure hills know it,
and the sky they inhabit,

that this is no metaphor:
those sentences of air
tight-lipped or breathy

still rove the horizon,
indiscriminate, reticent, there.

Nacre

Lucent, iridescent lustre, mother-of-pearl...

It sounds like its opposite: nacreous dark,
acrid flame, acid lake, sharp sand...

'This one I swallowed raw,' she whispered,
enclosing in his palm the parting

gift of an oyster shell, barnacled, chipped,
mauve-tinted, purple-edged, brittle;

and he thinks of her on the seashore,
sliding the oyster, silky, bitter, slick,

into her mouth, before she knew
this was the gift she would give,

before he knew he would lie here
feeling the shell's satin convex,

would conjure her soft resilience,
her throat muscles working the flesh,

the salt taste, to this more-than-parting,
to this lustrous white-out,

this nacred hell of ending.

The Bullet

You have killed something,
you don't know why –
deliberately,
though you did not know it.

Having nothing to say
but the whole bang shoot,
you made do with
glances and ricochets,

until one stray
returned, direct.
It rankles,
it works in and in.

You can feel it gutting.
The harder you hunt
the deeper it digs,
this bullet, entering.

Abstracted

To my surprise I wish you ill.

Inside my head you go your way
my way, you feel pain
as I would have you feel.

I talk with the ghost of you
who are not dead yet,

though you soothe with dead gestures.
Burnt on cortex and retina
you fade and fade.

So leave me to my idea,
my first and last things,

and this chaos
I shall call my oasis.
I shall live here as long as I like.
Not to forget. To be forgotten.

Quake

I am your skeleton.

Do not open the door, I might fall out.
Often you glimpse me through chinks
though when I rattle you seldom listen.

Sometimes I think I must have made me up,
a figment of bones, a construction to get you.

But no, I am your constant monster.

Though barely articulate
laughably I try not to fall in a heap:

I must say my say, I must
stay in one piece, I must keep going.

Therefore I turn on my heel,
I give you the cold shoulder.

So do not worry, I am moving
slowly away now – although
first I would strip you to the bone

and shake you.

Figment

I was your wish made flesh.

I was the years thrown down,
marbles for you to skid on,

I glittered and you dived,
I filled your hands and fled.

I come to you now as abstract,
I shift and shimmer, I hesitate before you,

I flutter, I twist, I turn away,
I shrink, I beckon, I come close.

I am the life you have not led,
I am the life you will not lead.

I give a shape to your imaginings,
I am not here except you conjure me,

I float before you in no retina,
I swim in the mind's eye.

I live before and after.

You do not let me
and I do not let you go.

We want it
and we do not want it so.

Relief

Past the last cadence surely.
The strain has gone out of it.
The tense instrument relaxes.

To whom do I talk if not
to you who do not listen
though I imagine you

in the auditorium
(no applause
bringing the house down)

feigning no recognition
of tunes wrung
from an old conundrum,

who exit as ever without
look-back or afterthought,
and compel refrain

that speaks to no one
without constraint or
equivocation.

The wrangle is over;
hear the words go
nowhere – and love them

the more for that:
somewhere is anywhere
and not to be trusted.

That's It

You re-assemble yourself with difficulty:

the torturer is away.

Simplicity is finished,
the world comes flooding back,

the evidence is destroyed,
no one who knows is anywhere near.

The smug silence of secrecy is over,
whoever wanted it to happen is gone

leaving behind no orders
and nothing to be done.

There must be others in the same position
but telling yourself is useless

for the feeling police are moving in
with whispers and razor blades

under cover of light.

Crowsfoot, there

in the mirror, in the flesh,
intransigent, inconceivable,
inevitable, incontestable,
inconsolable, ineluctable,

delta of elegance,
bird-print in the sand
beckoning:

all that is worth anything
is off the record,
to hell with paradise,
you have been here before,
clear the palette,
scrub out the blue

and come round to this
crowsfoot, this double life
carving its way down the cheek,
beauty and its opposite, and
let paradise go to hell.

Therapeutically Speaking

You have come to the end of the end. Thank god for that.
Go for it. First orders please,

something to take your mind off things,
then something to take your mind off that.

You could have been a figment of someone's imagination,
which is a proposition facing in several directions,

let's face it, but reduced to a subject, how does it feel?
You do not answer. How could you? Let me for you,

for these days you are not quite all there
and post-compositional tristesse has made you light-headed.

Is there life after poetry? Metapoetry
is on the increase, metaperson is in cold pursuit,

sub specie aeternitatis the whole thing's up for grabs,
and the rush hour of the gods is all the other way;

but the shemozzle somehow organizes itself
miraculously round the subject, me,

and in the surround-sound of emotion
you must not turn retrospective, brooding and gooey,

a feeling you might have done it all before and differently.
You have nothing to lose because you had everything to lose.

Static

The airwaves are glutted with sideways manœuvres,
bits of tryst, dribblings of tribulation,

fragments of haiku floating and jostling
with snippets of indeterminate peace treaty,

nuclear disarmament chatter, soundbites of love,
strands of jazz, syllables of bed talk, Darwin talking

at cross-purposes about origins with a cave-woman –
sweet and sour nothings evaporating in ether.

They speed by each other with no amen,

each solemn promise an exercise
in wish-fulfilment and delay. I find myself

among the privileged feelers talking in my head
to you out there listening somewhere.

But not really. You said *and anyway
there is too much to say ever to say it.*

Now there is too little.
It is less complicated that way.

We set sail on the hubbub of emotion.
We find our bearings.

I see us mouthing in the hiss and crackle.

Messenger

Fluff-ball waltzing
to your own music
over the floor in full view

of no one in particular,
delicate muzz
of absolute irrelevance,

puffed-up mocker
of gizmos and contrivances
(our ways of getting by),

soft wafter and drifter,
light conjuration
from crevice and wainscot,

dream machine moving
to the choreography
of a gingerly low art,

invertebrate evidence
of something or other,
incontrovertible

speck of diversion
sub specie aeternitatis with
applause unheard and

nothing
understood.

End Man

Talking is
talking beside the point,
is playing at the margins.

The point is
where by definition
you cannot go, where
may be void, may be

the nub of sense.

This is as far as I go
the man said meaning
literally that

as he stopped
mid-point and forgot
to admire the edge,
sea and sky, simply

all that was

to be negated by the simple
act of stepping out which,

wordless, cried out to be heard.

Gremlin

I am the static on the radio
I am the inkling
I am the sum that won't come out
I am the wasted time
I am the green grass over the hill
I am the shaggy dog
I am the echo on the telephone
I am the missing piece
I am the dream you don't recall
I am the fading PIN
I am the nutter on the internet
I am the *déjà vu*
I am the bubble in the windowpane
I am the half-formed thought
I am the *folie du doute*
I am the tic-tic going round
I am the bug
I am the *esprit d'escalier*
I am the blip on the screen
I am the quick bird of Caedmon
I am the Spooner Almighty – the Gun of Sod

I am the last resort

The Possible

The possible holds out her lovely looks,
The usual phrases form, the brain dissects,
All goes as it was never planned to go,
Without a hitch, and starts the gorgeous no,
That airy sky of blue anticipation,
That floating face, misty oblivion,
Where words are birds and flying is such fun,
Where ends have been, beginnings not begun.

Tomorrow will bring in its yesterday,
The serious words we never had to say,
And all the silly syllables we did,
Frolics on talky foam, the look of dread,
Spiralling spindrift between the here and there,
The seas of carefree and of everywhere,
To bring us to this pretty pass, these lines
Of self-denying nonsense with designs.

Still

The change from model planes
to girls, how clear it is
in memory: in still blue
it sputtered, cut out, curved
uphill and was gone. There he was

running over the Downs
for signs, a red flapping
of tissue tagged to a bush,
pieces of balsa, the fuselage
floating unscathed on a pool…

Instead, nothing. His interest
petered out. But when he hears
the bicker of diesel and a phased
drone over fields, part of him
is off, muddying trouser legs.

That last letter he wrote her,
was it wrongly addressed?
Still he likes to think of it
gathering dust somewhere
waiting to be slit open.

You and Not You

A truth is not the truth with you,
A lie is not a lie.
Truth and lies are what you say,
And what you say is you.

Today it's no, yes yesterday,
Tomorrow it may be maybe.
But it's all the same, you say them all,
And what you say is you.

Yes what you say is you, for me,
Forevers, nevers, maybes.
For you are what you say, I think,
And what I think is you.

PIN

I get my thrills from his delays,
forgettings, miss-tappings, his pure
absent-mindedness, his frettings
and digital lingerings,
his nervous fingerings, his decisions
not to press *Error* or *Cancel*,
his gettings in a muddle, until I say
Try Again, Carry on Regardless,
Hoping for the Best, Sorry
No Go, Withdraw, I'll Eat You,
Better Luck Next Time, or
Do You Want Another Service?

He finds me frustrating
and easy by turns.
I find him moving, quizzical,
in need of instruction.
He feels naked before me,
a bare forked animal
with too many fingers.

Sometimes he's trusting,
light-fingered, confident, at others
I resist his inept fumblings,
holding my secrets, teasing,
letting him guess, seeing
how long he can hold out
before he gives up or remembers.

I come to him slowly sometimes,
sometimes in a flash.

He's getting to know me.

Do Not Forget Your PIN.

Self Efface

Look at me is what
these poems I am reading
do not say so insistently
they reveal at every
turn of their lit
landscape their maker's
face he would avert.

Beneath these gleams,
these coruscations,
these glinting liquidities,
know the currents of the eye,
the heart's tight pulse.

She

haunts the High Sierra.

Men out of nowhere found her
cooking alone on the snowline.

With presence of mind or no mind
she tipped the pan, hot, on her head.

Hair hooped with spaghetti
she stared at them for dear life,

she, the loopy loner,
the spaghetti medusa.

Knots

I

Something not to return to finally:
unfakeable, ungraspable
abstract perfection.

Perfect it. I find myself
talking to you in my head
but of course you do not listen,
so I lose myself

rounding on you
who are not there
though in my head you are.
I round on myself therefore

asking, who is this
the more I turn to
the more you turn
into the creation of a need,

your lie my truth,
thin fiction, vacant sounds
rounding the silence with
absolute indifference?

Something not to return to, ever.

II

Heard in the head
how does it feel, to be
reduced to quotations,

to a subject, a sound,
a loudening echo, replayed
over and over, shrunk,

distended, distorted, mis-heard,
misunderstood, refashioned,
edited, finished off, rubbed out,

how does it feel, how does it?
– How silly of me,
you cannot answer.

But I make you.

III

A gift, this broken idiom?
Hardly. Astringent air,
wired-up and wary

jealousy of the full song
that turns saccharine,
is more like it.

Only at home in a
cantankerous music
of barbed curlicues,

of how love turns
to rancour, cankerous
consummation, never the

desired indifference.

IV

Knotted wrangle rather,
wiry laceration,
tangled coils against
an azure horizon,

against spendthrift
spindrift running riot,
blowing itself out
in sea fret and soured ecstasy

— something to salvage
from how love turns.

V

Knotty branches flare
in a pyre I warm myself by
with wry reflection,

contorted expression
of charred remains,
with ash in the exact

shape of a log,
its rings clearer now
in their death throes

poised to collapse.

VI

Knotted, knotty, knots,
the word has something
graspable about it,

how the tree, hacked about
and scarred over years
puts out these hard

protuberances, these
knotty expressions,
little defiances, in a show of

laughable dignity, fretful
snarls of self-importance, of self-
preservation and asseveration.

VII

To be given this
bracing gift of resentment
is some recompense:

hatred that distance denies,
silence suppresses
– that distance disperses,
silence forgets
– that distance defines,
silence amplifies…

The variations congregate.
The astringencies tauten,
the air grows thin.

VIII

After living it is time for words,
little transports of the equivocal,
even of the unequivocal,

even the unthinkably arrogant
airs of freedom, the radiant

spider's web that shifts
minutely, after rain glistening
with myriad translucencies,

holding to nothing,
pure and simple

– is the nearest you'll get to it:
nearly motionless, nearly breathless,

certainly no metaphor,
almost nothing, almost not

anything, almost
absolute abstraction.

from
LISTENING IN
(1993)

A Funny Smell

'It couldn't have,' said the rat man,
'Warfarin makes them head for the open, gasping.'
It had slunk under the floor to decompose.
Father: 'It's Brooke again, he's smelling'
– Brooke being the critic who had slammed him –
and we'd chorus it round the house, holding our noses.

Not the stuff of poetry, rotting rats.
Yeats turned Father down for the *Oxford Modern Verse*
with 'Too reasonable, too truthful. We poets
should be good liars... gay warty lads' – perverse:
at about that time Yeats was busy climbing down
to set up in rag and bone. Father harboured that.
His poems continued to ripple in subsong
over the backwater, feathering the inky currents.

As I remember this it all seems a lie.
Did we prise up the boards? Did the smell just fade?
When I was ten, for every poem I wrote
he promised me sixpence. After that I was silent.
Why is it poems kill people off before they are dead?
– every poem an epitaph and so on. Now he's not here
I'd bring him alive, warts and all. I'll pay.

the bar flies called him.
At seventy he still dived –
'Always get my head wet before my feet' –
and climbed the Deyá hills, goatish,
quixotic, tilting at something.
He raced me to the top, where he said
'A gentleman never pinches his best friend's girl'
which is just what I was doing, in secret.
So the old boy really is a wizard…

It was the idea of love spurred him into song.
What irked Father was not so much
stoogeing while the great man
went off with the latest goddess
as that he began to believe his own bunkum.

He took me vaguely under his wing:
wrapping me in his Oxford gown he said
'Now I'm going to tell them a lot of nonsense.'
It was no-nonsense nonsense.
When mid-lecture he tripped
into his poems, you didn't notice:
the art of irreverence, anti-rhetoric,
Yeats had nothing on it – the cool web…

For the last ten years his skull
swam in *the wide glare*.
Did a fly on his brain-wall
hear *the beating drums,*
the *old-world fighting* –
the duty to run mad?

He would have scorned this, cashing in on death.
My son, seeing his face in the paper, asks
'Is it Worzel Gummidge?' He'd have liked that.
'Difficult being in the poetry biz
with your dad,' he said to me once
(I didn't know till then that I was),
'I had that problem too.'

When someone complained to the local *policía*
that while he was sunbathing with his radio
a wild-haired man strode over
and tossed it, still blaring, into the sea,
they threw up their hands, 'That will be our
Señor Gravés,' and showed him the door.

Gaps

for Norman Cameron

Africa, three wives, a breakdown,
'those notorious gaps of non-being',
a heart-attack, World War Two,
psychoanalysis 'by a fellow-Scot',
a Catholic conversion –
he'd been through all that

by the time he sat me on his knee
and did *minnie-min-min*:
the spick shoes and turn-ups
at the end of my giggling drop
are all I remember of his visit,
and the clammy hands.

Adman, he didn't advertise himself,
and brought nothing back from gap-land
except 'Normal Norman' who solved at bars
the riddles of the universe
and dissolved the answers in hock,

who took *the voyage to secrecy*
but stays in the eye's corner.
Anguish writhes in his allegories of lust,
of how love turns: poems neat
as the trouser-creases I slid down.

I didn't know that sweaty palms
meant booze, or fear, or the big gap
he saw coming – or all three.

Mimsy

Metagrobolize meant homogenize
only not so smooth: not mix
as with paint, not pulverize,
but crumble, like soil.

Chum-ha was upright, blinkered,
tending to moustache, but harmless.
I had an uncle who was rather chum-ha;
he left part of himself in India.

'It wobbles a bit,' said Father,
trying the outside table. Shop-keeper:
'It vill vobble verse in ze garten.'
We called it the vobble-verse ever after.

Trigonometry took one second to say,
so it still means headache and temperature.
Try saying trigonometry
one-hundred-and-eighty times non-stop.

Umbling was shifting something heavy
little by little. Furniture is umbled.
When we moved house there was much
umbling and grumbling.

We sang the Great Panjandrum
to a psalm tune.
I loved its 'and so, and so'.
Only now is it a conundrum.

Gadgets

Write down in your own words what the poet means by...
'Means, my foot. It means what I bloody well wrote,'
barked Father when they set him for O Level prac. crit.

A student erupts in a seminar
'Why do we end up arguing what a poem's *about*?'
Touché; to fill the silence...

'And your suggestion?'
A poem should not mean but be etcetera?
A machine made of words, a sort of divine gadgetry?

Ambition was out, trust to inspiration:
over a bottle one evening, beneath his outdoor awning
Father set up a recitative:

'I shall go down for the odd limpid lyric.
Let's drink to that.'
As night closed in he opened up.

He was always making things –
stoppers for started bottles,
that bathroom contraption

whose rites I pondered, then gave up and asked:
it was to silence the tap water if his bath
needed a top-up with hot while the Third was on

– Heath Robinson affairs. Inspired arcana.

A Dying Art

The frontispiece to a book by my uncle –
a history of furniture – is a photo of Seymour
the gardener, England's last adzeman...

The long haft of the adze and his legs and back
make a quadrilateral. Hardly moving,
he chips the beam to a ripple of scallops.

But my uncle would slump in an armchair,
the daily grind done with for life:

he had not devoted his time to his first love,
chisel and plane, chamfer, hone and dovetail,
the art he learned in Paris in the twenties' wake,

and now it was too late, so I thought...
But on the day of his step-daughter's wedding
an oak chest appeared;

it bore two zodiac signs. Once, weeks earlier,
she had caught a glimpse of him carving it,
and knew there was no breaking off now...

His gift was reticent as a shell heard
only if you hold it to the skull and listen hard.

Mollusc

My father liked creatures with shells.
He had a pet tortoise
that hibernated under the bonfire;
the vet patched the hole with cement.

But his favourite was the snail.
He wrote a children's poem about it,
the tenderness, the slow silence, the timidity,
the persistence, love of the dark,
the greed. He called it 'she'.

———————

For weeks one summer they came out of the dusk,
covering the lawn, a beach of them.
You couldn't cross without crunching.
By torchlight I shovelled
all of them into water, salted.

The grey flesh bulbed to the surface and frothed;
the shells drifted down.
In a few days it stank.

In his poem he called them 'toppling caravans'.

Oxford

He was run over on Broad Street in broad day.
Was he dawdling between bookshops,
vaguely waiting to cross, like a leaf?

Was it suicide, or absent-mindedness,
or both? Never on time, he'd slip off,
hands fluttering at the threshold.

He played out the joke about dreaming spires.
Sometimes I think I must have imagined him,
imagined the rendezvous I missed

and remembered only six months afterwards,
too late. Willowy, nose up, he floats
in a dandified air, hovering at the edge.

Laid Back

When music came through the walls
you knew he was having an affair
with some idea, his spent butt

unfurling in an inch of Nescafé.
Laid back, he wrote his essays while Mahler
blasted and maundered in the background;

as he read them out the Mick Jagger face
looked profound, then bewildered,
then he'd rummage in his hair for something.

A stale tobacco smell and jeans
that had the same knee-creases for months
didn't seem to keep the girls away,

though they moved on fast enough:
was it sex in the head and art on the sofa?
His ambition was the theatre, stage-design:

he'd sit up all night over some miniature
card and balsa set, an airy erection.
His grand climax was 'Oh, Calcutta'.

Freshman English, USA, 1970

Someone talks about that dark spot
on the other side of the globe.
'Could you repeat that?' Or rather, don't.

We wrestle with clauses.
They put all their cards on the table,
even if they are blank.

When it comes to politics
I hold mine close to my chest.
Irony isn't their strong point:

several frown at 'A Modest Proposal';
I try to explain, but we find ourselves
falling back on attitudes.

One day the class suddenly shrinks.
Some of the boys are missing.
Silence. I feel hurt.

Someone blurts out 'Depression maybe:
yesterday their numbers were picked;
they could get the call-up.'

I can't think of anything to say.
We bend to our grammar. In the high
bunker-like windows feet are passing.

Making It

He taught me to say 'blacks' without blenching.
At his party I was the only white
but did my waspish best not to notice.
Though a student in my Freshman class,
he was seasoned. He showed me a thing or two.

'You press this button and look
the antenna goes up,' taking me for a ride
in his brand-new sports car which flew
along Skyline Boulevard. I bought his old car;
it looked like nothing on earth:

'I've got to sell it quick
for the down payment on my new machine.
By the way, you'll need this form,'
and he signs his wife's name.
Next day she phones: 'I want my car back, see.'

I blink and don't see. A week later:
'Keep it. I don't care, now I'm shot of him.
Know what he said? – "Well, if you wanna send
Gareth to jail, receiver of stolen…"'
and it all comes out:

'He ain't what you'd call a family man.
Forgot about our baby once and it fell downstairs.
I told him he was kinda careless. He agreed.
Rented himself a love-nest on campus
and used *my* name as security –

Story of my life. Fell for him over and over.
After all, he's charmin, you'd agree.
He even nicked some frat rat's tie-pin
to prove he'd been to college. So we married.
Now I'm paying for the whole of his damn education.'

Me lamely: 'At least he's made the best of it.
I mean the essays he did me were, well, rather good.'
'Yeah, and you wanna know who wrote them?
Love works in a mysterious way,
as you would say.

Anyway,' she ends, 'it's a fine auto.
May look a wreck but it sure goes.
It'll get you *all* the way back to lil ol Englan.'

Doggo in CA

When he arrived with a trunk of natty suits and winkle-pickers
we expected him to flower Gatsby-like on the lawn.
But jeans were anonymous; the trunk went back unlocked.
He came to California to shake off the dust of England

and the first person he met was me; I was part of the dust.
We never spoke about that. His classless society was exclusive.
His talk bristled amicably and was in quotations:
the struggle, bourgeois lackeys, capitalist imperialist swine.
In the early days the Lenin poster gesticulated over his bed.

He gave the impression that he knew where it had all gone wrong,
that he was lying doggo, meditating theories of action.
Meanwhile he got fatter, drank pots and pots of tea.
Grinning ironically he'd eye me with wire-rim specs –
steely revolutionary or just National Health?

On paper he was a tiger. His brilliant Marxist analysis
of *Sir Gawain and the Green Knight* had us all guessing.
He was a sucker for rhetoric, liked poetry that rhymed,
and could never square his ideas with a penchant for Yeats.
He had a large fund of rhyming slang.

When they swept up the stones on campus (ammo for students)
and built the law school like a barracks, he smiled 'child's play'.
He rented a room with the *Venceremos* underground, said it was
                                                            cheap.
The slogan for the hard Right and hard Left was the same:

'Outlaw guns and only outlaws will have guns.'
When police broke in and discovered an arms cache
my friend slipped out the back. He said he was shocked:
he didn't know it was there, and anyway something could have
gone off. He should know: his dad was an ex-copper.

His silences grew – in spite of an ear operation.
Did he feel the fault-line opening, truths beyond talk,
the dialogue reduced to an internal Pacific roar? –
while the tea intake increased and he sank
into his thesis on 'European Novels: the Social Context'.

Once a week he'd launch himself down the freeway
on an ancient Raleigh for an all-you-can-eat-for-a-dollar lunch.
He made clandestine trips to England to pay last respects,
then secretly married for love and a residence visa:
we aren't sure if in that order; nor I think is he.

High Life

It's 'Gigi del Fuego'. Someone giggles.
'Now boys and girls you'd better be good
or I'll show you the lot.' Cries of 'nuts'.

The tough-looking bouncer is an odd shape
and the waitress, is she, is he...? I'm uncomfortable,
ambivalent, but sit glued, my palms sweating.

Those palmy days of cabaret and cancan
are chipped pilaster, moulting velvet,
a chandelier that has dropped its tears,

and the audience sits in corners, abandoned
each to himself, herself. All's topsyturvy.
Gigi, topless and barefoot, dances poker-faced

on bare boards in a circle of lit kerosene,
then juggles two firebrands and runs them up and down
those slicked limbs, wriggling as the flames lick.

We are inflamed. If the place went up
no one would know from the charred remains
who was who or what was what.

I see through to the skeletal dance.
We are sexless in our old charnel house.
Nothing is what it seems, including my laugh.

The Cockroach Sang in the Plane Tree

The heat of the moment,
the cold stare, the lovers' tiff,
shall cover the earth. All of you,
legs, lusts, nerves, good feelings, good looks,
genitals, hearts, hurts, shall ascend
and spread, shall keep on going round.
No one shall start again.

No torso shall get caught in the act.
Your last meal, petrified in the throat,
shall not be analysed.
You shall be a flicker on the scan,
a shadow punched in concrete.
Your DNA shall give its last twist.

'The end of civilization as we know it.'
You won't know it.
There shall be no 'unthinkable'.
All shall be thinkable,
atomized to a thought.
All shall be vapid.

Anything goes because everything shall go.
All shall be level, shall be up in the air.
No tone shall be suitable.
There shall be no tone

when the dust settles
forever and forever.

Travels

'Avez-vous vu Honolulu?' –
his voice would modulate,
relish the syllables,
their shimmer and shade.

I made a cave under my bed –
its legs on books, all round it
a dark curtain of blanket –
to swot up his prep after lights-out.

Twenty years on,
grass blades are nudging through
the hole burnt by my midnight light bulb
in our spread rug. Honolulu, Honolulu…

Out of Season

Last night when I hung my dark
green home-knit sweater
on the bedroom doorknob
to block the line of light
from the half-landing, that phone call
to the intimate-voiced hotelier
came back – 'Of course sir
I'll send it at once, we wouldn't
want the lady to miss it...' –
and our coming down early
into the winter garden,
a leafless tree afloat
with persimmon lanterns on the sharp
Western air and the ground-
mist about to dissolve.

Umbilical Cord

When it came to the bit about cutting it
I passed out. Scripture was Passovers,
Crossing the Jordan, Flights into Egypt,

with stop-offs for extra-curricular
activities like sex and birth
that couldn't be squeezed in elsewhere.

When they picked me up off the floor
I wobbled and was lionized
a whole day for turning to jelly:

'What's it like then, fainting?'
Like nothing. Not sleep, not dreamy wings;
but dead minutes, a blackness.

———————

'And that is, er well, what it is':
he goes pink and points to the one picture
we've all been waiting for,

then flicks to the next slide.
We are anaesthetized.
A diagrammatic baby, still-born looking,

flashes up on the screen. No one faints.
We hustle out of the classroom
shadow-boxing our way to the playground,

the rough and tumble. We are men now,
ready for the hard stuff: warnings not to go
'below the belt', roam Soho.

———————

Prospective dads sit round looking green
at a demonstration of deep breathing:
'hold and count, relax, hold and count,

relax.' A plastic football is urged
through a large knitted tube.
This is 'the birth'.

I try to keep my head but end up
putting it between my knees,
then fiddling with a window for air.

The final event is a home movie:
the last push, blood, slappings, first howls.
Miraculously, I breathe free...

Take a deep breath. Now for the real thing.

Going Blind

i.m. James Reeves

1   *Look, No Mirror*

In a corner of our garage
lurks his medicine cabinet
I thought would come in handy.
It smells as strong as it ever did
of his potions and lotions,
and mostly of his electric aftershave.

His desk had a hook
which carried the wire from the plug
to his shaver. Each morning before work
he'd fish the Remington out of a drawer,
plug in, and then lean back
to a contemplative buzz.
He did it all by feel.
To get the sideburns
he'd place an index finger across,
then shave up to it, like a ballerina
tucking a flower over the ear.

I never saw him look in a mirror.

2   *Notching*

He must have made my letter rack
about five years before I was born
when he could see clearly:
it has tricky joints, and only today
I discovered a sliding panel.

'Get yourself something to do.'
'I want to do woodwork with dad.'
I soon graduated from watching
to lending a hand. When was it
he stopped making things on his own
and needed me there, though he never said,
and when did I begin to do it all myself?

Our *pièce de résistance*
was an electric-train table.
His instructions for the canal and bridge
were precise. Then we had to saw
the whole thing in half to get it up the stairs.

I'd guide his saw-hand
along the thick lines –
'A little to the left, over a bit' –
stopping him to blow off the dust
and see where we were going.

3   *Sticks*

An earthenware stand by the front door
bristled with sticks. Every house had one,
I thought. We played pirates
with the umbrella stick, whipping it out like a sword,
strutting with its telescopic case held to the eye,
jousted and fenced with the knotty stick,
the smooth one, the never-used lethal
shooting stick, and the one with the rubber stop,
the Landrover model I sawed an inch off.

My sister has the stand;
I have the sticks. Though scattered,
he moves among us crabbily –
walking stick oblique, Chaplinesque.

4   *Touch Type*

Fon'y mskr my houdr yout nsdr
sd you fif lsdy yimr
– jokes in Jabberwocky, neo-Lilliputian,
a sort of pseudo-Urdu, I thought,
until I decoded it:
Don't make my house your base
as you did last time,
the left hand one key to the right
for the whole paternal letter.
On my next – flying – visit
I noticed his H and G were green:
he'd peer through thick lenses
to check the green keys
were between his index fingers,
then he'd cock his head and was off,
no second look, no proof-reading,
brain, to fingers, to postman, to reader.

When I was five and he was forty-three
for months a large chart of the keyboard
hung over his desk. I thought that this
must be what it means to go freelance.
The chart was going more and more out of focus.
Other people's dads went out to work,
mine went upstairs
where for two years and £1000
he wrestled with a fat international
conspectus of World War Two writings,
his first commission. Home-front peace
was broken by orders from on high:
'Turn it down, I'm earning your living.'

The Home Guard was the nearest
they'd let him get to the action.
He was guarding a signal box
(in case the enemy shunted along?)
when he woke to someone shouting

'Wake up, the war's over.'
He must have rubbed his eyes and blinked
at daylight on three sides.

After a morning's work
he'd sit back for his eye-drops.
The first one usually missed,
then a bull's-eye.

The typewriter accelerated
from popping to a battery.

5   *Listening In*

He had a Talking Book.
One year the whole of *War and Peace*
followed him round the house.

He also had talking people,
readers paid to be toneless:
'Why *will* they be expressive?
Actors manqués – so are most actors.
Let the words do the work.'

Mother was an expert Wife to Mr Reeves.
She read *The Times* letters after lunch
every day, without taking in a word –
his window on the world:
he liked to keep in touch, at second hand,
and was a fan of the first-cuckoo-of-the-year type.
He started an interminable correspondence
about Proust's madeleines – 'how could
his imagination have been fed
on such dull grub?' – and was sent recipes
and even a box of madeleine-like biscuits.

Milton was too ambitious, he said.
He liked his high art to keep a low profile.
Much of his day-labour was spent
chiding ambition. In the dark hours
he'd nod off in his armchair
and wake to the ticking of a run-out LP,
then struggle upstairs
to write a lyric in thick felt-tip.

6   *Artwork*

He'd like to have been a painter,
he said once – more sociable than writing;
painters can chat while they work:
the Artist in his Studio, a nude or two,
people milling and posing.

In galleries he twisted the keeper's arm
to let him take his stick:
'short sight, you know,' leaning
toward some detail of an Old Master.
Once he got carried away
and pointed a stick at a nose.
Attendants homed in from nowhere.

When I was eight he pasted his children's poem
called 'Others', about moths and mice
and crooked brown spiders, in my autograph album
and framed it with darting creatures.

If my children ask me to draw something
I can manage a spider; that's about all.
His sketches grew sketchier...

7   *The Entertainer*

It's an octave short, no good for Chopin,
Schumann, Liszt – not that he liked them much
(my girlfriend went off at both ends) –
and Beethoven could be a squeeze;
but it fitted his eighteenth-century favourites,

though he played it less and less as the keys blurred.

It glints, a metallic green, promising
1930s cinema schmaltz.

Our piano-tuner twinkles 'Was your father
an entertainer?' Well, yes
and no… the man he might have been:

velvet curtains glide
and he rises through the floor
in a black-and-red striped
smoking-jacket, white hair
edging the collar, a live cigar
perched on the piano lid
in which his face appears
relaxing to improvisations
as his hands blindly
spread the effortless chords.

8   *Pentels and Smells*

THICK ENDS FIRST the injunction
on the underside of a home-made
collapsible table I've inherited,
and a cookery book says
COOKERY BOOK on the cover.
He was always labelling things in black.

He bought Pentel felt-tips by the dozen
and kept them in cigar boxes.
When he lit up he sign-wrote the air.
The smell still whooshes out of his books,
which are labelled with an *Ex Libris*
quotation from Lamb: 'Borrowers of books,
spoilers of the symmetry of shelves
and creators of odd volumes.'
Once he stuck it in one of mine.

Going through his things
we came across a list of numbers:
National Insurance, Pension, NHS, tax code –
across the top in crabby capitals,
COMRADE REEVES.

9   *Pots and Pans*

His territorial sense grew sharper
as his sight blurred,
especially in the kitchen:
'Where have they put the bloody sugar?
Can't they see I can't see.'
He took up cookery when mother died,
puffing Hamlet or Manikin
through thick and thin
to what he called wallpaper music,
monotonous classical,
speakers in every room.
Dinner-guests had to ignore
the ash-log centred on the mousse,
the slug in a fold of lettuce,
and enjoy the washing-up afterwards.
They came for the badinage;
the food would have to do.

From America I sent him
The Large-Type Cook Book.
His thank-you carped 'not large enough'.
I reclaimed it when he died
– getting my own back.

10   *The Great Fire*

'Help fire fire' flapping across the lawn
and down the street in pyjamas. What are they doing
leaving the poor old man in the house
all on his own like that? You ask him.

He woke in the early dawn to a smell,
thought the house was ablaze, and beat it.
He'd gone to bed two hours before.

Smouldering... Rooms with doors ajar
got soot-stained; the rest were untouched.
At the centre, his arm-chair,
the winged family heirloom, tasselled in gold:

he was nodding late at night to Schubert
when the stub in his right hand
declined in a twitching arc.

The chair was replaced with a fireproof
imitation leather thing, bolt upright.
Above it clacked an extractor fan
but he drew the line at smoke-detectors –

they'd be detecting him all the time.
The plastic lampshades, which he myopically
thought were attractive, had melted.

Sitting beneath bare bulbs he said
he looked like an ad for Shelter –
a study in black and white.

Half my things are his. Peninsulas of soot
have crept over matt boards. It won't come off the books,
and even today I find mono LPs
with WARPED across the sleeve in felt-tip:

the stylus rises and sinks,
the music lurches and there he is
squiffily leaving a half-full whisky
and swaying up to bed in the small hours.

11   *Daily Bread*

Shopping was a campaign:
up one side of the High Street,
each kerb and level known by his stick,
then the difficult cross-over –
'Why are they so damn quiet these days,
they creep up on you,'
as he vaguely parried a car –
then down the other, shop by shop.

But when he passed you by, in summer
beaked with a green eye-shade,
he had not necessarily missed you;
he did not want your guiding hand
or to stop for a chat ('If you say
"How do you do" they go and tell you');
you were seen through.

12   *Deus ex Machina*

When the train stopped
he jerked awake, panicked, stepped out
the wrong side onto the tracks
and found himself sprawled on a sleeper,
the electrified line inches away.

So he took to sleeping
to the end of the line.
If it was the last train,
the Drunk Special – not that he was –
he went back ten miles by taxi.

Is there a god of the blind? –
an inscrutable all-knowing
taxi-driver who ferries shaded men
in a limousine past irrelevant countryside,
with stereo background and a switch
to turn the world on/off.

13   *Tentacles*

Over the years my hand ended up
in the downward position
and he wasn't tugging, but being tugged.

This wouldn't do. Gradually
I was guiding him by the elbow,
but only at critical junctures

and at exactly the right speed,
his other hand holding his stick,
an extended arm, feeling, inching…

Our eight limbs went spidering
over the web of the pavement.

14   *Douane Syndrome*

I don't look at you:
one eye goes through you,
the other goes right past.
They spent years trying to get me
to make a rabbit jump through a hoop

and told me I could earn £10 a day
as a guinea-pig. Finally
they gave my condition a name,
and let me go – incurable,
but not at any rate father's glaucoma.
He said that before the war
they didn't have a clue and botched it.

I have his magnifying glass.
My children like to play with it.

Once I saw his eye through the wrong side,
the pupil dilating.

from
REAL STORIES
(1984)

Stills

i.m. Mary Reeves

I

The photo of you I have
by heart: you in a deckchair
casting a clear shadow
on garden flagstones where
crab grass has not yet pushed through.

Poised, smile faintly bewildered,
you are enduring something,
watching past my shoulder
a landscape I know well:
sea-glint, green estuary,

oxbow, a distant hill;
behind you a French window
with silvered panes, ajar
to a dark inside, where stilled
shapes are about to stir.

II

Often when I think of you
it is that photo, taken late.
After your death
he can't have thought of you
like that. He resurrected
a portrait done in your late twenties
when your mind was on soldiers
and Ceylon; you took him on the rebound,
he said. He heard of you
through friends, a beauty,

unobtainable – until he got you;
after that he was your slightly stern
stand-offish schoolmaster,
a change from the others, he said.

Your version doesn't exist,
except in silence:
your hands stopped
over some household task,
an absent look.

III

From this distance you are,
I suppose, not as you were
but as I would have you.

I recall sun on a window sill,
you silhouetted, reading novel
after novel. Did you live

in books, in those quiet
mid-morning lulls you had
to yourself? – that life I touch
only as photographs.

IV

Italy – a chance to indulge
your liking for canals and cannelloni,
Canalettos, Guardis, madonnas,
Caravaggios and pietàs!

Your son-in-law may have
chased her round the Trevi Fountain –
the bottom-pinching sort
whose short mamma stokes him

with spaghetti done al dente
as an antipasto, and remembers
all the others her carissimo
brought home without getting hooked –
but here it was, your first
grandchild, a squalling six-month-old
bambina. You must have sighed
as you cradled it
in your English arms.
In a few days you died.

V

Your body from Italy, mine from Greece
to a homecoming I did not want;
yours in the hold, mine

hanging in air, all movement
gone, all thought but one,
an absence that clings,
a solid cloud, through which

the plane plunges and rocks
till the ground comes up
and we bounce and skid to a dead
stop amid rushing silence.

from REAL STORIES (1984)

Theme and Variations

'The Harmonious Blacksmith', the only piece
I ever heard my father play –
he must have been practising it
when his sight failed. His hands spun
elaborate and endless variations,
filling the minutes, the half-hours
it took my mother to 'get ready'.

The tune comes to me for no reason,
as do the endless streets, the increasingly rare
car-less byways we trailed in foreign cities,
looking for the right café, quiet, no wind,
waiters polite, where he would practise
the difficult art of whiling away time,
waiting for small inspirations from passers-by
or from the couple two tables away
on whose conversation he would speculate
in a loud *sotto voce*,
making me squirm or sit rapt
by his inventions of episodes
in other people's lives, until his talk
was stunned into silence by the traffic,
or the light went
and it was time to guide him
down blind alleys back to the hotel.

The Mentor

Tending abstractions in your
prismatic head, your hand stroked
back imaginary hair.
Always anxious to shatter
some fine ray of truth, you kept
us listening through dinner.

Ash lengthened; fingers yellowed.
Arguments were hot, and you
switched sides quicker than it took
to take one swallow of your
well-cellared liquor. After-
dinner sleep came fast to all
but you, who mulled the subject
over with quiet laughter.

In this book now I have you
arguing with yourself, or
anyone. I read into
the night, and sentences blur.
Smoke fills my head; I recall
your jovial evenings.
On the page your phrases bulge
and swallowing them is hard.

It was shot off giving the thumbs-up
as he led the charge over the hilltop;
he also said, since it's gone
it won't get hurt at the wicket
and makes a good excuse for lost catches.

Brandishing the shiny stub, prodding
the air, sometimes our ribs, with it,
he could still grab with fingers
and flexing palm the nearest ear,
nose or shying shoulder; and once

he got my hair: the tuft
glinted in his fist, then floated
through dust-motes to the floor.
Mother took me to the doctor
with suspected early balding; even now
my silence makes me scratch my head.

He did General Knowledge, the bullet
head jerking to quizzes on rugger,
stalagmites and -tites, the last
country to leave the Commonwealth,
on how many rivers called Ouse,
on populations of unlikely places

where he'd never set foot and didn't want to.
Stubbly moustache, eyes that poked
into a diminishing future, visions
of touch-lines and boundary fences,
he made a virtue of sanity

and was slightly off his head.
There he is, running up to bowl
in a deep green limbo, fingers
feeling the seam for off-spin or googly,
in a blue funk at the endless
journey across his elysium.

English Lesson

He is our fond teacher.
'This is where it happened, this
is the place.' Stopping where
Perdita gives flowers to Florizel

he stands, legs slightly apart,
and remembers how they took him
one noon from the P.O.W. reading club
mid-speech... Before the war he was engaged;

after it, he soaked in the bath for hours
slicing dead skin from his soles,
it is rumoured: shoes wore out
fast on the Burma railway.

When a shovel disappeared
someone stepped forward to own up
and was shot then and there;
then the shovel turned up...

Stories for schoolboys –
his high-voiced and bitter
charity made real, I see now,
in the listening, childish faces.

Out of Bounds

Always the several entrances:
from the hall where we had pep-talks
on team-spirit and prayers after chips,
through a door at the back, past yards
of parquet, into that quiet;
or the garden passage, or the never used
dark stairs from the attic 'squealers'
down to the ground floor – the high
voices of his daughters floating up.

The feel of other lives next to our own:
a First in Modern Languages, then travel
and marriage to a neat Frenchwoman:
only once do I recall him letting fly,
about 'that blackamoor who blew a bubble
in the front row of the House photograph.'
He dreaded the day his daughters would arise
as beauties on a sea of scrambling schoolboys.

He did not survive the car crash one summer
somewhere in the Massif Central.
His family did; they were sucked back
into France with their memories: bemused
on the sideline in a surge of pent-up boys,
mother and daughters watching as bare limbs
jinxed and tackled across an English pitch.

Can We Interest You in God?

'Do you have a Bible in the house?'
'My husband has written a new version
thank you' she says, and firmly shuts the door.
Craning over the banister, I'm proud.
Could your mum come up with a line like that?

'See me afterwards, I'll tell you my method'
the chaplain says. So I go. 'Leaving us soon
for the big world, are you? Remember God.
Where to now?' 'A month or so in Paris
before I go up.' (I'm pleased with that last phrase.)
'Er... take this *A Prayer a Day*... try not to...'

What's he thinking of? The *Moulin Rouge*?
Plastic macs in the Latin Quarter?
That's nothing on the boy at school
found naked under another boy's bed: 'Oh Sir,
you see Sir, I lost my way to the loo.'
He was expelled for that caper.

My dad's *The Holy Bible in Brief* –
I don't think he believed a word of it:
he cut out the difficult bits
and stuck to the story. Never mind the meaning.

End of Term Report

'Let me see… the name is…' turning
the pages. 'H'm, not getting any worse, not getting
any better.' Still turning, 'Ahem.'

Ahem. He dilates on how
he can tell the character of a chap
from his performance on the rugger pitch.

Play the clarinet? 'I have a son
who conducts. Fine thing, music.'
He shoots out a hand.

This is goodbye. I flinch:
his little finger's missing. Grasp it.
Otherwise you've failed the test.

The Graduate Trainees Take Off

'Get yourself a drink.' I fumble
the bottles, take a sip, and wince: it's gin

and soda... I try not to be noticed.
He tries not to notice: 'And how are things

in Mailing?' (Nothing to write home about.
Last week someone grabbed his brolly

and left – to go to the Gents,
so he said. He was never seen again.)

At the round table each thinks of the quest,
something to say. No food comes:

he grips the edge (a breakdown? a fit?),
but relaxes when the salvers arrive.

A silver cover lifts off – to reveal
supine potatoes. After the meal

we are stranded on the carpet,
high flyers, herons on one leg.

Where he clutched the table
I spy a hidden push-button.

Regret

People my verses do not teem with hurt
more than the fleshed-out memories
that get to them.

Past words, flesh-touches clutch,
recede, leaving the mind
blanker than mind can contemplate.

I would be Aeneas
but the shades that haunt me
do not turn to marble. They wander

formless and forming in the mind still.
I have tried Lethe and the upper air;
each time regret pushes me back again.

Central Valley, California

for Steve and Marsha Shankman

The centre-line flicks at me
and rebounds in the rear-view mirror.
I drive my appurtenances,
slant-six and battered body,
my headlights out of whack –
but it's not night now –
my raucous Plymouth, bent
and patched-up piece of America,
into this desert valley.
The antenna shakes as the wheels
judder over the cracked tarmac.
The broken-down radio,
its loose connections jumping,
bursts into life, goes dead, bursts again
into a Savings and Loan ad, 'guaranteed
federally up to forty-thousand',
then a baroque sonata.

I drive past mountains
bristling on the skyline with dead trees,
hillocks in the foreground
stippled with browns and greys,
past tentacular roots sticking out of the sand
and rocks wind-tortured into fat
birds, faces of old men, noses, a hand:
a bombsite in the sun's equal glare,
a landscape ravaged by the eye.

There should be ghosts here
and I try to see them:
of pioneers, of gold-prospectors;
and those who stalked invisible paths,
ghosts of a ghosted race, with whom I share

too little of their trampled rituals.
But it's no good,
even the word 'ghost' seems out of place.
No one is here; unreal
America spreads its wavebands
over a desert air.
My alien eye
conjures a violence from nowhere.

Rat Race

'Stroke it. Stroke. Don't
for God's sake let it go.'
Too late. It clawed, drew blood,
rapped and skidded on vinyl,
then skulked behind cupboards.
'That one'll be nervy
for at least six weeks now.'

Our neighbour had a wife and a white
rat that slept in the bottom drawer,
usurping underwear and socks.
Rats in a maze: he couldn't bear
to make the sleek albino
chase cheese down corridors of wire.
The landlord ('pets forbidden')
never saw the rat. It was too quick.
Eventually our neighbour was evicted
for painting a giant eye
on the bedroom window – to stop, he said,
the couple in the apartment opposite
peering in.
                    His research topic
was overcrowding. When the cages
bulged rats, would they fight,
turn cannibal, make love, go mad?
(He said he could tell a mad rat.)
From this, of course, the human situation.
But we are no more rats
than naked apes, I thought.
Then he escaped to a Tanzanian
rainforest to study the chimpanzee.

I think of him in his old
oil-squirting car, cruising the Bay Area's
tangle of freeways: the sun-glinting steel,
the bumper-to-bumper drone,
eyes behind glass deliberately
not looking into other eyes,
friendly, unseeing, alone.

California Sounds

A drop-out Sociology Ph.D.,
the walls of his clapboard shack
lined with all the books
he had not sold yet ('they make
good insulation') and a squat-dog
pioneer stove with the flue
straight up like a cocked tail
to keep him company –

he meant to retreat, to think and write
about the individual in society,
and came to ground in a sea
of field grass and hay stubble,
seed misting the horizon to a brown haze.
He listened to his thoughts and the bamboo
shifting, the sharp leaves
scraping together, hedging him in…

Finally he made it into print
in *The Last Whole Earth Catalog*
selling hand-whittled Shakuhachi flutes
world wide. He sawed and reamed and trimmed,
then sat cross-legged for days
perfecting his embouchure
until the thin notes were suddenly there,
easing and bending from the stout bamboo.

The last we heard he had jetted
across the Pacific, a Shakuhachi
contract in his breast-pocket.

Pugilistic

He knocks his man down nimbly,
knowing by knack the exact spot
to put his foot for the gliding fulcrum,
brain in his fists and brawn compacted
to the logic of a direct hit.
And now he meets the lens, the hullabaloo –
no rebounding from slung ropes
or bouncing on the balls of his feet,
so he parries with an 'I am the Greatest'.
But words won't work for him
a shield of fisticuffs. He looks
baffled for an instant, eyes and face
open to all hurt; then the chin
comes up, and the bludgeoning grin.

California Drift

A bobbing aluminium
Beer can nudges the river bank.
Across the shallows the deep wood
Absorbs a moody thrum:
Someone plucks at random –
No serenade to bodices
Bowing from a rabbit-warren
Forty-niner's brothel, now
A hotel of exhausted beds.

The girls are asleep for good.
Eddies glint and blur:
The moon is panning gold.
Voices of guests behind clapboard
Fade out and in, soothe and threaten
Like a low-power radio,
Making sense but not in words.
It could be any language anywhere.

To the left an empire died
In the heads of a few Russian
Sea-dogs who nosed the coast
For years, inlet by inlet:
Vladivostok, the Aleutians,
Fort Ross, Vancouver, Anchorage,
Eureka, Mendocino, Manchester...
The wide Pacific edge.

When in the prematurely dark
Bar on the main drag a man
Mooned at us, we walked out scared
Into a silver light that shone
On boardwalk, shack shop, grey fir trees,
The square head of a nineteen-fifties
Gas-pump, pot-holed macadam;
A deer was levitating in
The headlights of a slowing car.

TO HELL WITH PARADISE

The can gurgles and settles. Soon
The sun will come up on the right
Having crossed a continent
In one day, the yellow miles...
Okies and dropouts drift
And fetch up here. All night
They tap their frets and hum
To themselves their marginal tunes.

Melting Pot

Green scars glimmer in El Camino Real's
architectural overkill: Spanish stucco
massage-parlours rub shoulders with ticky-tac
Tudor steak-houses and Disneyland motels:
the Cinderella Inn is a giant shoe.
The President once helicoptered over:
'And when light industry replaces orchards...' –
the royal way! 'Survivors will be Prosecuted'
jokes a No Trespassing sign. We hope it jokes.
LUV U.C.B. – or else – is a car's number plate.
A feminist collective sells home-made ice-cream
with frozen smiles. Above the hot macadam
banks, bars, realtors, poolrooms, waver in the pyre.
Next to a Szechwan restaurant a green billboard:
'Invest in Ireland, Europe's Silicon Valley'.
H. Salt & Co., sporting the London Underground
with a map that has no blue Victoria Line,
sells wedges of Iceland cod in cardboard trays
printed with the Gothic, front-page-personal *Times*.

Avenues of palm, of Indian catalpa,
Australian eucalyptus... Outside our house
a primitive ginkgo waves its Japanese fans.
The Dutchman next door fishes below the snowline
in lakes called Honey, Josephine, Suzie, Big Jack.
Wobbling at the top of a telegraph pole
he shouts down, 'Here in America you are free
to make your own electrical connections.'
Jewish, they came over when the war started;
her father was an undertaker. Much remains
unspoken between us. Our German landlady
turned up after the war, the husband before it;
it is said that he preferred his bachelor days
on the porch steps with his bottle and squeeze box.

There's a grown son by her first marriage, silent,
eyes unfocused, head shaven and to one side.
The attic has a tin trunk lined with *Der Führer*,
'38, picturing kindergarten children
perfectly behaved; in the letter pages
English blimps from Malta and Beaconsfield
make overtures in German translatorese;
and on the cover, there he is, saluting,
looking exactly like his caricature.

Pepper Tree

Green globes I crush and smell…
On the other side of the world
Domestic peppercorn
Stung my nostrils until
Vague islands swam in my veins.

No wind, no ripple shifts
These delicate, barbed leaves
Like fishbone-skeletons:
Fish out of water, spines
Bared to a steely sun.

A Slawkenbergian Tale

'We're writing an article on sons
of well-known dads. Can we do you?'
'But that's like interviewing someone
with a bent nose: it's something you can't help.'
(No *esprit d'escalier* now, for once.)
'Er... well... can we print that?' 'No.'

I'm violently doing the twist
with a girl I've never met before.
Drink splashes the floor. 'You went head
over heels and landed on your nose'
she is saying as I come round, blood
blossoming on her frilly white blouse.

'A hairline fracture. An operation
wouldn't work. Breathe okay? Good. That'll be all'
and out I go. 'At least there's the girl'
I think. But she only liked men
with bloody noses. Today mine's slightly bent.

Silence

Two in a room. Two in a room, and silence,
Except for a steady creaking as she writes
And the slowly turning pages of his book –
She does not ask the title, being gone
Far away with friends he does not know,
Talking across a table, which becomes
The table where she writes about her life
And his, versions he might not recognize;
And when he looks up from the page she's not
Someone who sits there writing, but a girl
He conjures up inside the room, and he
Is not there either, but inside the book
Open on the desk on which he leans.
They are alone, not as two lonely people
Who talk to stop the silence, but as two
Joined by the silence between them, in a room
Whose only sounds define the lack of sound,
The wordless space enveloping them both.

For Carole

Too young for memories like these,
Of girls I never got,
And of the few girls who got me…
Is this how the rot
Sets in, the mind crumbling around
The life unlived, or lived badly?

This is the threshold then, marriage,
Where the stories vanish
Into vistas of blank page
On page of married bliss.
And we are young; prospects for age
Are even hazier than this.

Those memories! – such poor
Attempts in candlelit soirées
To dazzle would-be girlfriends; or
Those times when, feeling bored,
I sagged beneath a rain of chat.
I wonder that we ever met!

And yet we did! – and still we meet
Daily in these areas
Of silences and doubt, no treaty
Signed. My thoughts retreat
Sometimes to past certainty.
I know our love is incomplete –

And will I hope stay so. Completion
Has no renewal. I wish
I could say this more openly,
Bring my words to a flourish.
But love is a truce sometimes,
A continuous meeting each other half-way.

Paediatric Ward

Those who never made it
into the open – whose last
breath was oxygen that had not
slammed doors, rustled leaves,

who gave up the ghost
with hardly a gasp –
cluster to the pane, noses
pressing the glass, hands

waving less and less.
Down corridors the childless
wear masks; you can see them
any day in the street

not window-gazing,
eyes straight on as if
to meet someone they
know will not be there.

Stone Relief, Housesteads

Mediterranean, alien,
stone-flesh chafed
and chastened, whipped
by wind, by hail,
dissolved in rain, till legs
shrank to spindles
and quiver hung
awkwardly from shy
shoulders – or did
the carver's bare hands
shiver, and the chisel
stop too soon?
However it was,
this meagre figure
is our knock-kneed Diana,
our uncomfortable, chill
madonna of the North.

Blind Pianist

His posture is listening –
not to a landscape of images
where notes rush in rapids
and a waterfall, then dwindle
in high trills to a stream,
where octaves are vistas,
and darkening passages
lead to the eerie minor –
but to the sound alone
where dark and light are tones
without colour. He leans
into his mirror of music,
his ruminant medium.

Church Wall

Strands of an organ voluntary, the lonely
practice of a Saturday, float
from the church, tangling
with traffic and pungent street-smells.

This wall of shining flints has no rules.
Masons, skilled at knapping, once tapped
flints with patient trowels, feeling
for seams, and split them with no effort,
accurately. They reveal
shapes that come as in dreams,
known before, unrecognized till seen.
It is a skill trained and intuitive.

Each irregular stone-face is a rounded
hollow or rounded belly,
and holds in its centre a sun:
in many incarnations one sun shines
along this wall, that, lithe as flesh,
flexes and flashes beside the raucous street –

rough harmony that breaks, and swells again.

TRANSLATIONS

Horace I, 11: *Tu ne quaesieris*

Don't ask, you must not know, Leuconoë,
About the end gods give to me, to you.
Don't fool with horoscopes. Take what comes.
We may have many winters, or our last
Now tires the Tyrrhene sea against the rocks;
And so take thought, take wine. As life is short
Prune back long hopes. Time, jealous of our talk,
Goes. Gather the day. It may be your last.

Horace I, 37: Nunc est bibendum

Now, friends, drink,
now beat the earth with free foot,
now with Salarian feast furnish the gods' couches.

Once it was wrong to raid
ancestors' cellars for Caecuban,
once, when the queen, with her rabble of eunuchs,
those virile adventurers,
drunk with sweet fortune and madly daring the world
made crazy ruin of the Capitol
and a grave of empire.

Return of scarce a ship from the fire's roar
diminished her mania. Caesar sobered her
whom Mareotic wine had made mad.

He fettered that monster of fate; she
sought death with nobility.
She did not shudder at swords like a woman,
nor did her ships retreat to hidden shores.

Calmly she risked a last look at her flattened palace,
steadfastly clutched sharp-toothed snakes
that her veins might drink deep the dark venom;

no lowly woman, she,
ferocious now death had been fixed on,
scorned to be led by barbaric Liburnians
unqueened in arrogant triumph.

Catullus 2: Passer deliciae meae puellae

Sparrow, my girlfriend's truelove,
playmate she likes to hold in her lap,
and give her finger-tip
to provoke your sharp nips,
when my seductive darling
likes to play strange games with you,
and even, I think, satisfies her yearning,
quenching her passion: ah sparrow,
I wish my playing with you as she does
would soothe my achings also.

A selection from a sequence of about seventy quasi-dramatic mono-logues 'spoken' from beyond the grave by the Russian composer Dmitri Shostakovich. Hindsight, self-justification, guilt, and the tricks of memory, all play their part in the psycho-drama. The sequence reflects 'the Shostakovich wars' sparked by Solomon Volkov's compelling but terrifying book *Testimony: The Memoirs of Dmitri Shostakovich* (1979), which claims to consist of interviews with Shostakovich but is now generally considered to be a collage of anecdotes and memories that circulated about the composer. Were his the politics of conformity, resistance, or survival – or a tense, ultimately inscrutable, tangle of all three? In the words of his friend the diva Galina Vishnevskaya, 'His only real life was his art, and into it he admitted no one.' One of Shostakovich's favourite Shakespearean characters was Lear's Fool, who speaks unpalatable truths and calls the king 'nuncle'. Hence my title, *Nuncle Music*.

Revolution is the getting
of a different set of noses
into the trough, with a few idealistic
outriders to lend authenticity.

Composition is the getting
of a different set of noises
into the air, with a few hedonistic
flourishes to fend off authority.

———————

Listen, I give you sound.

Make it yours, the whole gamut,
guts fondled and scraped,
squeals, welts, efflorescences,

salves and lacerations, wrenches, jerks,
twists, whines, spidery attenuations,
tensings and relaxations, snarls, snaps,

writhings, retentions, releases,
retchings, brittle disintegrations,
acidities, grips and gripes, floatings,

slidings, slitherings, ironies,
pulsations, inscrutable insinuations,
amplitudes, harmonics, sardonics,

twitchy, spiky, gimletty, gritty, grabby,
strung out, composed in a rush, overwritten,
underwritten, remote, close to –

and the dips
suddenly over the edge like

falling awake in the dark.
Quicksilver,

untranslatable.
Alive at any rate,
at any rate not dead.

This isn't music this is electricity,
eat it you must eat it
every demi-semi-quaver of it.

I follow the labyrinth
into the muddle,

I see a boy
sabred to death by a Cossack,

I hear my art
cut to shreds by the deaf.

———————

The future, it will blow over,
but who put the stars there?

The withering away of illusions takes forever,
like rotting teeth.

But you can pull out a tooth.

This ache becomes me,
I don't know when it started
or if it will stop with me.

They say not to be wise after the event.
But there is no after,

I am the event,
it goes on inside my head
still, over and over.

I shadow-box with myself:

let's have no more patented saviours,
no Stalins, no Solzhenitsyns,

and no more me.

————

Bloody Sunday?
I can do you a Bloody Sunday.
Every Sunday is bloody,
every Sunday throughout history,

some year, some where,
nineteen hundred and blah blah blah,
here, there, bloody everywhere.

All Great Men would penetrate
the cerebral cortex of history,
the Ox butchers the people, my violin-squeals
insinuate themselves into your brain cells.

The dictator's wet dream means blood on the floor.
I pray not to come back to life sometime
spewing harmonious tripe for self-preservation,

belchings of the spheres, gargantua for the masses.

————

For some reason everyone speaks quietly.
Every toady expects a miracle.
Stalin will give birth.

They agree, carefully and quietly,
today the Great Gardener will give birth,
the man with the mighty moustache
and the withered arm will give birth.

This music is not melodious,
not aesthetical, not harmonious.

The composer bids farewell to his score,
to his career, perhaps to something more.

———————

One-ski, two-ski, three-ski:
*We spy an anti-person artist,
non-realistic, formalistic.*

*Music, music,
it must be definitely authentic,
it must be absolutely authentic,
it simply has to be authentic,
it must be definitely gorgeous,
it must be absolutely gorgeous,
it simply must be gorgeous.*

*It must be optimistic,
it must be realistic,
optimistic, realistic,
realistic, optimistic.
Optimistic is realistic,
realistic is optimistic.*

– not, decidedly not
music futuristic, ironistic,
pessimistic, modernistic.
For that is death all round,
and all-round death stinks.

Light music with a vengeance,
the heaviest light you'll ever hear,

cod for the Ox to swallow.

———————

Hamlet farts through a flute,
I fart through Hamlet.

Everybody farts
through somebody else,
and the Great Ox farts
through everybody.

Harness slow, ride fast.
Think slow, write fast.

They play me so hard
I can't keep up.

Listen two and two make five
because they say so

and you say it after them
and I say it after you
and my music says it after me
and everyone says it after my music

and I know it's all lies
and you know it's all lies
and they know it's all lies
and everyone knows it's all lies

and my music knows that too.

I fart through my music,
I fart through art.

———————

Devils, enemies of the people:

cows moo, dogs howl and moan, horses neigh.
Does the enemy of the people admit that…?
The cow is silent. They stick a spear in its side.
The cow moos. *Guilty, it admits it is guilty.*

Silence is a sign of guilt, so is mooing.
Bonfires. Overheated executioners.
Which is the beast, which the man?

Art aspires to the condition of music.
Music aspires to the condition of silence.
Silence aspires to the condition of death.

So art is death. It is very simple:
if our Leader doesn't write music
or books, or paint, but cuts people up,
his art is butchery.

That thought keeps your trap shut
– or opens it in whispers,
in bars, at street corners:

you die today, and I'll die tomorrow.
It is beautifully symmetrical.
It is called being a patron of the arts.

Feel the wheels turn,

watch ex-prisoner and informer
bow to each other across the foyer,

see the silhouettes appear
and disappear along the corridor.

———————

We live in the dark
and I'm learning to see in the dark.

Up with mediocrity.
Up yours my music says.
I am not mediocre:
I wear thick specs.

I stare at Tchaikovsky
and he stares back.

(The Boss is on the phone
letting his henchman my interrogator
have it: one bully does for another.)

The classic and I study each other.
Suddenly I am dismissed
to a brand new life.

Ever since that day
I can reproduce Pyotr Il'yich's beard,
every hair and fleck of it.

As for the dark,
I can see as far as the next man,

which is not very far
to judge from the number
who disappear into it.

———————

Suddenly I am absolved.
The Great Man shows mercy
with an extra dose of madness.
I am rehabilitated.

I have been shafted over and over
but now I am to be considered a virgin.

It's simple, so very simple.
I am a person again.
Again I am a person.

An Historical Decree
does for an Historical Decree.

History's a whore,
it lies like an eyewitness.

But please, no posthumous rehabilitation.
Somehow I still don't feel like a virgin.

Composers must master one instrument at least,
piano, piccolo, it doesn't matter.
Even the triangle.
Surely the Ox can manage the triangle.

Look at him there in the back row
fixing the conductor with gimlet eyes
counting the rests – plenty of rests
for the glinty triangle.

When the Great Ox rests
you know he's up to no good,
writing edicts in his head
about the historical necessity
to do for discord

with the help of a purge or two if need be.
The Ox's trill. His thrill.

Gagarin sings my song in space.

Mine the first notes ever up there
dwindling beyond the stratosphere

forever while we go on dying
and the unborn turn to dust

to revolve in their eternal
interstellar interludes.

Dwindle dwindle little star
dwindle in the minor

degrow like a jellyfish,
thin to radiant plasma,

echo to lovely nowhere.

Gagarin sings beyond the skies
intergalactic platitudes.

———————

The bigger the lie the more you'll get the point.
Russia is the homeland of elephants.

I overwrite, I rant, my music rants, it lies.
Truth-tellers live in fear,
conspirators do their stuff in the loo
then flush for authenticity.

My music flushes for authenticity,
it flushes for authority,
it's obvious if you've ears to hear.

I flush for my music,
my music flushes for everyone,
all of you, the whole shooting match.

Every note I write is a send-up:
my huge C major goes
so over the top you won't believe it
– and you mustn't, ever.

Music is a weapon in the struggle.
That is the sort of thing I'm expected to say,
and I say it,
gigantomania unheard before.

I disappear into it,
vanish in the flash of a baton.

Now you hear me now you don't.

————————

Freshly baked odes to the great and the wise:
it'll be hot but I can't vouch for the taste.

We're all replaceable. Behind your back
feel your replacement ready to screw you, numerous
nameless nobodies waiting for the signal to sit at your desk
and write your novel, your symphony, your poem.

The Master of Harmony calls us all screws
in his miraculous machine, his harmonious
euphonium, his euphonious harmonium.

Red Beethovens spring up out of the blue.
One screw does for another just like that:
from today you'll be a genius screw,

and so you are. Anyone can become a hero here.
Gogol's *extraordinary nimbleness of thought*:
Excellency, give the order and I'll switch over presto.

Any day a bright new screw, a shiny Shostakovich,
could appear and I disappear. Yesterday you were the best,
today you're no-one. Zero. Zilch. Shit. Screwed.

Change your address, maybe they'll leave you alone.
Ghost composers people the provinces,
musical slaves in the sticks writing sweets from shit.

Life is better, life is merrier, sang the Bovine Almighty,
then in some remote spot had the lot shot.

Some days I wonder if it has not
happened already, if I am really here,
if I have not disappeared,

and who speaks to you now is not a figment,
his song sung and story over
in slow diminuendo.

I've screwed the pitch so high
something has snapped, I've snapped.

When is a figment not a figment?
When it's a figment.

————————

The sky is dressed in a gendarme's blue-grey trousers.

He stares at me from my desk, and I bin a symphony.
Great chunks of the man's life missing, Mussorgsky,

who brought bent backs and trampled lives
into our music, who dodged the sleuths of history,

one of those dolls that won't knock down,
idiot lying low to bob up again and again,

agreed with you as far as the door.
Then carried on.

————————

The delicious word death, my foot,
tell that to the corpses
grinding their way to whatever place
beckons with open jaws.

Death makes it all happen I suppose,
the music and the paint and the words
that stave off the inevitable,
the deranged Gangster
grinning at our navel-gazing,
this going round in circles, artistic,
unrealistic, formalistic, autistic
solipsistic circles.

All the art in the world,
full-throated or only pretending,
however crafty, shifty, sly,
cannot outwit death.
Death will gnaw our twisting arty entrails,
and declare them delicious.

How good that there is no one left to lose
and one can weep, writes artful,
artless Anna. We weep all right.
But fifty million ghosts remain to be lost
to the Great Ghost's ravening maw.

What can she say?
That she is living in a lunatic asylum,
that we are all crazy,
that the Gangster's mad?
– but then no one would hear her again.

———————

One day a sparrow flew into my dacha
and shat on my unplayed score.

If a sparrow dirties your creative work with his,
that's no great matter. Much worse
is when it is done by personalities
more significant than the sparrow.

Voices of the disappeared, voices of the dead,
their strangled cries tie my guts in knots.
They bear no witness except to the ghost brain,
their small noise echoing amongst my bombast.

They watched our Leader's face for clues,
then shat in their pants with a great load.
The lucky ones were taken out, wiped down,
brought back. The unlucky were taken out.

The Sublime Doodler makes us do that.
The bigger the grimace the greater the load.
Imagine it tipping the scales
against those weightless souls

who could not stomach the smell, who sank
up to their necks in it. But I,
I contained myself, I tell you.
That is what you are to believe.

I rant like this to not go mad,
to suffer the ordure, to not stink, not to be
one of those who ever stank, or sank.

————

The grave straightens out the humpbacked.
Unfortunately corpses don't jump out of graves.

A man with no memory is a corpse.
A man with too much is for the chop.

Somewhere in between
is where most of us live.

The corpses carry on with their lives.
So many pass by. You must leave them be

for they are me
but somnambulant sans music.

I don't know if I'm happy,
I don't know if I'm sad,
but I make music,

unlike those who feel by rote,
who have been brain-washed
and heart-washed and wrung out.

Is the dance with death any nimbler now?
Fears are dying but are not dead yet,
chants the visionary, revising poet,

but a dying fear is a ghost
gliding to the land of the dead,
a segueing corpse.

Treat with irony what you hold most dear.
Things you love too much perish.

——————

So is the weather here always like this?

I just listen to the music.
Either I like it or I don't.

Music is wordless.
That's why I'm still here.

These days I'm a walking mummy,
a resurrected pharaoh.

Everyone whispers and stares
waiting for me to go for good,
to disappear into their idea of me.

My idea of me is simple:
there is none, there is no idea.

I write what I write,
I do not have to have a reason,
I do not have a reason.

Absolute uncertainty, granite incertitude,
flinty absence, call it what you will,
my notes don't come in bottles.

That is why I like the future:
it isn't, it does not exist,
it is a figment as solid
as the earth I stand on.

———————

Prithee Nuncle,
shall I live, shall this music live?

Today I would make silence.

Silence is forbidden in St Leningrad.
On the streets of that city
there is noise of joy perpetually.

But silence would get inside me,
nuzzling and groping for entry.

Father, what if they hang you for this?

Do not worry, they'll make a fake,
a replacement with knobs on.

How many notes does it take to die?
How many notes does it take to return?

No chorus, no soloist, no apotheosis,
just music, where you will find me
ducking and weaving.

I like it so that no one can hear
except what they choose.

What's it about?

What's it ever about?
Work it out for yourself,
make what you will of me.

You won't know what I thought,
you won't know what I felt,

I do not know myself
though I thought and felt enough.

I am not here,
throw in the earth.

It trickles still.

Notes to 'Nuncle Music'

p. 113 'Listen, I give you sound'. This poem ends with the memory of an incident Shostakovich is supposed to have witnessed during the October Revolution, when he was eleven.

p. 114 'The future, it will blow over'. Solzhenitsyn thought Shostakovich was a stooge. Shostakovich thought Solzhenitsyn was messianic.

p. 115 'Bloody Sunday?' 'Bloody Sunday' in Soviet history refers to an incident in the First Russian Revolution (1905). In the sequence Stalin attracts several names, most frequently 'the Ox'.

p. 116 'One-ski, two-ski, three-ski'. Much of this poem is a rendering of Shostakovich's 'anti-formalist' skit *Rayok*, which literally means 'small paradise', and by extension a fairground peepshow. Shostakovich is supposed to have written this (for private performance!) after the devastating denunciation in *Pravda* of his opera *Lady Macbeth of the Mtsensk District*. 'One-ski' etc are cultural apparatchiks.

p. 117 'Hamlet farts through a flute'. Shostakovich wrote the music for Grigori Kozintsev's film adaptation of *Hamlet*.

p. 118 'We live in the dark'. One of the bans on Shostakovich's music was suddenly lifted, for no apparent reason. 'The Boss' is Stalin.

p. 119 'Suddenly I am absolved'. 'The Great Man' is Stalin.

p. 120 'Gagarin sings my song in space'. 'While orbiting the earth the Soviet cosmonaut Yuri Gagarin sang a song set to music by Shostakovich.

p. 122 'Freshly baked odes to the great and the wise'. 'The Master of Harmony' and 'the Bovine Almighty' are Stalin.

p. 123 '*The sky is dressed in a gendarme's blue-grey trousers*'. The first line quotes Mussorgsky.

p. 123 'The delicious word death, my foot'. The first line quotes Whitman. 'The Gangster' is Stalin. 'Anna' is Anna Akhmatova.

p. 124 'One day a sparrow flew into my dacha'. According to *Testimony*, composers were known to behave as described here when Stalin (a keen doodler) was 'auditing' their work.

p. 125 '*The grave straightens out the humpbacked*'. The first line is a Russian saying. The 'revising poet' is Yevgeny Yevtushenko.

p. 126 '*So is the weather here always like this?*' The first line is one of Shostakovich's characteristic non-committal comments when asked for an opinion about a new composition by a young composer.

p. 127 '*Prithee Nuncle*'. St Petersburg was renamed Petrograd and then Leningrad by the Soviets. This poem has Shostakovich's version.

Index of Titles

Index of First Lines